Basingstoke H

The Early Story of Old Basing

Mary Oliver

The Early Story of Old Basing is the sixth title in the Basingstoke Histories series. Details of how to obtain BAHS publications can be found at *www.bahsoc.org.uk*.

Basingstoke Archaeological & Historical Society

© Mary Oliver 2024

Published by the Basingstoke Archaeological and Historical Society
(Charity no. 1000263)

www.bahsoc.org.uk

First published 2024

All rights reserved, no part of this publication may be reproduced, stored on a retrieval system, transmitted in any form or by any means, electronic, mechanical, photocopying, recording or otherwise, without the prior written permission of the Society.

ISBN 978-0-9928074-6-7

Printed by Dolman Scott Ltd, Thatcham, Berkshire, UK

Front Cover
Part-restored greyware jar from Basing House (photo by B. Large, courtesy of Hampshire Cultural Trust)

Acknowledgements
I am grateful for the help I have received from the Hampshire Cultural Trust (formerly Hampshire County Museums Service) for permission to photograph items in the collection, to past staff and particularly to Ross Turle and Jenny Stevens; also to David Hopkins, County Archaeologist, and his staff past and present; to Butser Ancient Farm for permission to photograph their reconstructed buildings; to Anne Thom, Finds Liaison Officer for Hampshire, to Surrey County Council, and to Chris Rudd Ltd, for permission to reproduce photographs; to John Pearce and to Colin Richards. My chief thanks go to BAHS for giving me the opportunity to share my interest in the village, which has been my home for so long, with Society members, and friends and neighbours in the village. Special thanks go to the Publications Committee, particularly to Ginny Pringle. Also to Barbara Large, Penny Potter and Robert Applin for photographs and to Alan Turton and Stephen Oliver for drawings.

The Early Story of Old Basing

People have lived in Old Basing parish for thousands of years. Before written records, our only evidence comes from archaeology of different kinds. Archaeology is such a dynamic subject, new discoveries add to the evidence, and new scientific techniques add extra information about old finds, so there is never the full story. There have always been unexpected discoveries of antiquities, which in the past were regarded as great curiosities and little understood until they aroused sufficient interest in scholars to study them further, and now archaeology is a very complex science. The story of Old Basing, village and parish, has benefitted from various kinds of discovery – the field walking expertise of Mr Willis, founder of the local museum, and his flint-collecting friends; the commitment of Lord Bolton, descendant of John Paulet, defender of Basing House in the Civil War, to uncover the remains of Basing House between 1875 and 1910 when archaeology was in its infancy; the revealing aerial photographs taken after WWII and since, the work undertaken by professionals and volunteers prior to building and road works from the 1960s onwards; and the recent 'Dig Basing' test pit survey of village gardens undertaken by the Basingstoke Archaeological and Historical Society (BAHS) from 2014 to 2017 – all these and more will feature in this story.

Diggers hard at work in their test pit in The Street (photo by BAHS)

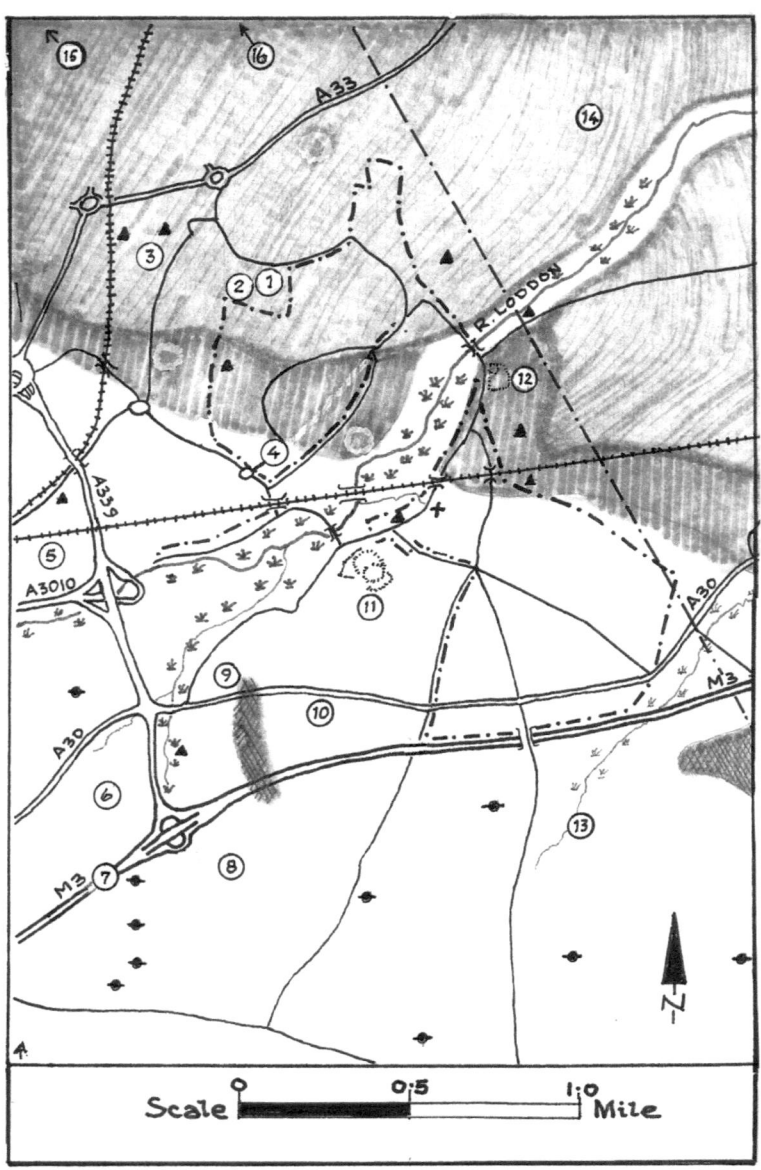

Archaeology of Old Basing and Lychpit area (drawn by A. Turton)

Archaeology of Old Basing & Lychpit Area.

① Gt. Binfields Copse
② Daneshill
③ Brick Works
④ Cowdery's Down
⑤ Basing View
⑥ Ructstalls Hill
⑦ Common Plantation
⑧ M.S.A.
⑨ Wellocks Hill
⑩ Crabtree
⑪ Basing House
⑫ Oliver's Battery
⑬ Huish
⑭ Lodge Farm (east of)
⑮ Merton & Marnel
⑯ Razor's Farm

☐ Chalk   ▓ Clay-with-flints   ░ Alluvium
▨ London Clay ||| Reading Beds

◆ Sites From Aerial Photos.
▲ Stray Finds.
—·—·— Boundary of Developed Area of Parish
——— Route of Roman Road

It is unfortunate that no early maps of the village survive. The earliest map is the one drawn up for Lord Bolton in the 1760s by William Godson, who also mapped Basingstoke and Odiham. Much documentary evidence, which would have been of enormous help in tracing the history of the village, was lost in the fire which destroyed Basing House after the siege in 1645. It is clear from the Godson map that the village then as now basically consisted of a street running along the rising ground above the floodplain on the south bank of the river and this looks like a long established pattern, with a centre round the church, another round Basing

House, and one by the Bolton Arms. There have been occasional archaeological discoveries in this continuously occupied settlement area but larger scale work has taken place in the surrounding parish and this adds to the picture of Old Basing's development.

The geography

The setting of the village, in the river valley of the Loddon running roughly west to northeast through the village, is favourable for settlement. There are several springs which provided an ample supply of clean drinking water, and there is a small tributary valley to the south (now followed by the M3 link road to junction 6) which joins the main branch from Basingstoke in the marshy area alongside Redbridge Lane. Other tributaries, including Petty's Brook in the north of the parish and the River Lyde rising south of Huish, all flow into the Loddon which eventually joins the Thames. The Loddon drains the chalk downland, providing natural route-ways and fertile land on the alluvium of the valley bottom, though the extent of marshland at various times has limited the number of suitable crossing places. Patches of clay-with-flints on top of the chalk remain in a few places, particularly at Crabtree Plantation, part of what were once more extensive deposits. The chalklands form the majority of the parish, meeting a narrow band of the Reading Beds (a series of sands, clays and gravels) and beyond them are the clays of the London Basin in a line running north west/south east through the village (as shown on p.2). The patches of residual clay-with-flints on the chalk were harder to cultivate and often remain as woodland, notably an area at Crabtree Plantation.

This varied geology provides a variety of soil types which has considerably influenced the land use of the parish. The lighter, often quite thin, soils over the chalk bedrock have been favoured for arable farming since the introduction of farming. They would have supported a less dense cover of vegetation, and so been more easily cleared for cultivation. In contrast, the heavier tree cover of the clay lands would have been much harder to clear, especially with primitive ploughs, but when they were settled, the soils did support both crop growing and pasture. The sand and type of clay that characterise the Reading Beds were also found to be suitable for brick and tile production.

The distribution maps of archaeological finds show a marked contrast between the chalklands, with the majority of finds, and the claylands to the north, with a much scarcer pattern, and this is true of other parishes with similar geology. However, it is likely that the bias of searches in favour of the chalk, and the cropmarks seen from the air of sites on the chalk being much more visible than those on the heavy clays of the north, have affected the apparent distribution. Certainly recent fieldwork ahead of development in the north of this area has shown the heavy clays to be occupied in later prehistoric times. The position of the village, straddling this geological divide, gave it the advantages of both the gently rolling cultivable downland and the forests offering timber and game and later, good farming land.

First signs: the Palaeolithic

The earliest evidence for human activity in the parish comes from the Old Stone Age or Palaeolithic period, which lasted an almost incomprehensible length of time, from over 850,000 BC to 10,000 BC in Britain. Over this lengthy period, the climate was subject to dramatic changes as ice sheets advanced and retreated over northern Europe, with warmer intervals between. In one of these warmer periods, there is evidence for a tropical climate in the Thames valley with hippopotamus and hyena found beneath what is now Trafalgar Square! These extremes in temperature affected the landscape and sea levels, with much of the water being absorbed in the glaciers, resulting in the rivers cutting deeper channels in order to drain to the lower sea levels. In warmer periods, when sea levels rose again, natural erosion led to the build-up of sediments in the valleys which were cut through again by the rivers during the next cold period so that terraces were formed. They are studied by geologists and archaeologists to build up a dating sequence for this period of extreme change.

Early people discovered that flint was one of the rocks which could be fractured in a controlled way to give sharp edges for useful tools and weapons, and the river gravels and the clay-with-flints deposits on the downs were both useful sources for this important raw material. Fortunately flint survives where organic matter decays, and flint implements provide the best source of evidence for these distant times. Even so, there is limited evidence for human activity in this period, and especially *'in situ'* – which means where it was originally deposited. For much of this time Britain was not very attractive for settlement, and our ancestors went to and from the continent according to the conditions as Britain was still joined to it.

The population is thought never to have been very large; the hunter-gatherer life style requires a considerable size of territory to maintain a group of people. In these distant times people were an earlier form of human than the current one, and there are no actual remains from Old Basing. There are very few from the country as a whole, the nearest evidence being a sturdy leg bone and a tooth from Boxgrove in Sussex, preserved under a cliff fall some half a million years ago. This covered the land surface where a group of people were dealing with the results of their hunt, and preserved *in situ* the flint debris from the knapping work being carried out there. In one case this flint debris has been painstakingly put together again to reveal the shape of the finished implement – a beautiful handaxe. The handaxe is the defining tool of this period, referred to as Acheulian after the place in France where they were first recognised as deliberately made tools. As the name suggests, the handaxe fits comfortably into the palm of the hand to make it easier to perform tasks such as skinning an animal, digging for roots, cutting vegetation, or cutting up food – in fact a Stone Age Swiss army knife! There are variations on the shape but the most common ones are pear-shaped or oval, with sharp edges. Modern flint knappers can turn one out in a relatively short time, and it can probably be assumed that our predecessors could too. The evidence from Boxgrove gives a wonderfully vivid picture of this group of people working together, skilfully making the tools they needed for the tasks in hand.

Flint is commonly found on the chalk downs of north Hampshire, with some areas particularly rich in large nodules. There are some in the parish, notably the clay-with-flints deposit along the ridge at Crabtree Plantation, but more survived on the surrounding downs and would have been utilised by those early people. Finds of flint implements of this date on the downs were assiduously collected and recorded by Mr George Willis and his friends Mr John Ellaway and Mr Herbert Rainbow (Ellaway & Willis, 1920; 1934). They collected finds of all periods (but particularly loved the flints) and the collection formed the basis of the museum in Basingstoke, which opened in 1931 supported by an initial grant from the Town Council. Mr Willis was its first honorary curator, helped by Mr Ellaway. Later the museum was taken over by the County Council who supplied permanent staff, but Mr Willis kept his interest right until his death in 1970, visiting often and bringing exhibits for the wild flower table and interesting items given to him.

Wellocks Hill

The one major site these flint-hunters found in Old Basing was south of the village itself, where Redbridge Lane leaves the A30. The slope of the valley is quite marked at that point, continuing across the main road to the slope by Crabtree Plantation. Here there were available flint nodules, a ready supply of raw material, and available water – the branch of the Loddon at its foot, later utilised for Upper Mill water mill and more recently for watercress growing. The site is referred to in the literature as Wellocks Hill (after the 19th century miller) but is now better known as the Lime Pits leading onto the Common. The site was extensive, stretching along the western slope of the valley leading up to Ructstalls Hill, now part of the Black Dam housing estate and no longer in the parish. The hillsides with the water below would have made good hunting grounds for catching prey as they came to drink. There are very nice handaxes and other flakes from Wellocks Hill (Ellaway & Willis, 1920) and more finds could still be discovered from this area; a worked flint flake was found in a rabbit scrape near Crabtree Plantation in 1996.

A handaxe from Wellocks Hill
(photos by B. Large, courtesy of Hampshire Cultural Trust)

There is one further implement from our parish which comes from later in the Palaeolithic and was discovered during the excavation of a later site at Cowdery's Down (Millett & James, 1983). This is a small handaxe found in a runnel in a patch of clay-with-flints which was made on a flake rather than from a core, and has working on both faces. It dates from the phase of the Palaeolithic associated with Neanderthal people which in Britain was some 50,000-30,000 years ago.

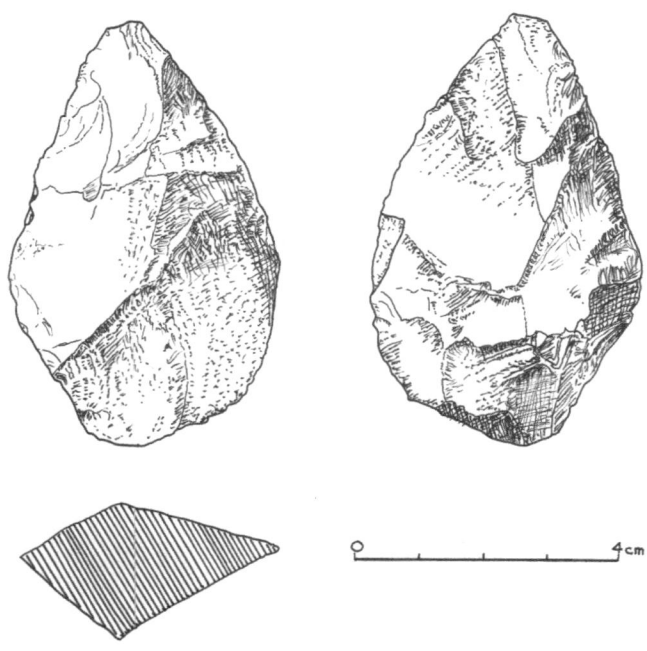

The small handaxe from Cowdery's Down, both faces and cross section, (redrawn by A. Turton from Millett & James, 1983)

Remains of this human ancestor are more frequent than earlier ones and although in the popular imagination the Neanderthal has been seen as the archetypal cave man, recent work has amplified our understanding of these people, who were a successful form of human over many centuries. They were more robust than '*homo sapiens*', our current human species. Ultimately they were not sufficiently adaptable to survive into modern times but certainly co-existed for long periods and some of their DNA has been traced in people in this country and others. New research has shown that they probably were able to speak, they had the use of fire, they buried their dead and most recently of all, some cave art has been assigned to them. They were so like us that it has been said we would probably not give them a second glance in the queue for the bus!

There is no surviving local evidence for the latest part of the Palaeolithic, after the ice had retreated for the last time. By this time, people were anatomically modern and their tools were more advanced. A large variety of flint implements were manufactured on flint flakes. The great examples of cave art on the continent were made by them. Paintings could not survive in our damp climate, but there is engraved art in the caves at Creswell Crags in Derbyshire and other examples of carvings on bone and antler tools. Our nearest examples of material from this period are from Hengistbury Head in Dorset which overlooks the Solent, which would then have been a river running through a valley and quite reachable for hunters and settlers from what is now northern France following the herds of deer and other animals.

Changes: the Mesolithic

As the climate continued to warm, sea levels rose and Britain became separated. The vegetation gradually changed and steppe vegetation was replaced by more temperate species, including trees. Much of the country became covered in forest, which offered a wider range of foods - nuts, berries, fruits, roots and leaves - to be gathered. The animal species also changed to adapt to these different conditions and so did the lifestyle of our ancestors hunting them. The smaller game living in the woodlands required a different hunting technique with different flint implements. Bows and arrows became the favoured weapons. This new flint assemblage is called Middle Stone Age or Mesolithic and lasted for many centuries, from *c.* 10,000 BC to *c.* 4,000 BC. The characteristic tools of these hunter-gatherer people were axes, hafted for use on the timber of the forest, and microliths (small flint flakes) which were used to arm arrows and for many other tools and implements.

Their axe heads look fairly rough and ready, but they were very practical – they could be easily sharpened by taking off an end flake at an angle, and so are called tranchet axes. Large examples, probably used for digging, are often referred to as 'Thames picks' as they were first discovered in the Thames valley. They would be hafted onto a wooden handle and secured with a natural cord or organic binding. Detailed knowledge of the environment and the useful properties of all the plants and trees would have been taken for granted, learned by trial and error and passed on to their successors. Information about the best sources of stone, including non-local outcrops, would also be passed on from generation to generation.

A tranchet axe from Wellocks Hill
(photo by B. Large, courtesy of Hampshire Cultural Trust)

The other characteristic flints of this period, the microliths, would have been mounted onto a wooden shaft and secured with a natural resin, no doubt with a feather flight for balance, and shot from a wood and twine bow. The size would have varied according to the prey. The style of microlith also varied according to area and date. Our Mesolithic ancestors favoured river valleys for hunting, again because of animals coming to drink, but also because of the water fowl and other riverside game. Evidence from elsewhere indicates that they were also efficient fishermen, making fish traps from woven wattle, and their carpentry techniques enabled them to hollow out tree trunks to make log boats. Again, the best evidence from this parish comes from Wellocks Hill (Lime Pits) and neighbouring slopes, where numerous flint implements have been found, both by Mr Willis and his friends (Ellaway & Willis, 1920) and by later searchers.

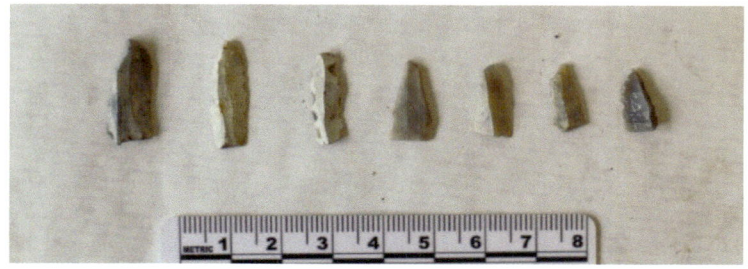

Microliths from Wellocks Hill
(photo by B. Large, courtesy of Hampshire Cultural Trust)

Many microliths and microcores (from which the microliths were struck), and tranchet axes and also flake tools – multipurpose scrapers and engraving implements for working bone and antler – have been discovered over the years. It seems likely that the banks of the river were utilised further north too – a tranchet axe was found during the building of houses in Priory Gardens (pers. comm. M Oliver) – and in some of the test pits excavated during the BAHS Dig Basing project some late Mesolithic material was found. In one test pit near Oliver's Battery, microliths, a core, a fine blade (see p.12) and blade fragments were discovered (Pringle, 2020).

Close by, another test pit yielded a quantity of burnt flint, which may have been associated with heating water for either cooking or 'sauna' like activity. Mounds of burnt flint, found close to water, have sometimes been dated as early as the Mesolithic but more frequently to the Bronze Age. One of this date was recently excavated prior to building near The Hatch (Oram, 2006), and another on Greywell Moor, excavated by BAHS, in the same situation, beside a river, was undated (Peryer, 2016). However, a large concentration of burnt flints in Penrith Road, Basingstoke, beside one of the springs feeding into the Loddon, was investigated by Mr Willis in 1912 when construction was taking place, and he thought it was a Mesolithic cooking site because of the associated flints (Stokes, 2008). It is tempting to imagine a communal feast beside the river after a successful hunt!

A small amount of flintwork was found in some of the other test pits along The Street, enough to suggest further activity along the edge of the river in this period. No doubt the area was visited at certain seasons when foraged foods or game were particularly prolific, and then the groups would move on to other parts of their territory. With their skills in working wood, they would have been able to construct shelters where and when needed and any necessary containers from basketry or skin. There is no reason to believe that they would not have had a complex social organisation and traditions, but of course, all the organic materials at their disposal – the wood products, fibres, skins, fur and leather which could have filled out the picture – have not survived. However, it was a successful way of life which continued for many centuries and still just about survives in some parts of the world. Although local evidence is slight, it is in line with evidence elsewhere in the county, showing these ancestors utilised the resources of the river valley as part of their mobile lifestyle.

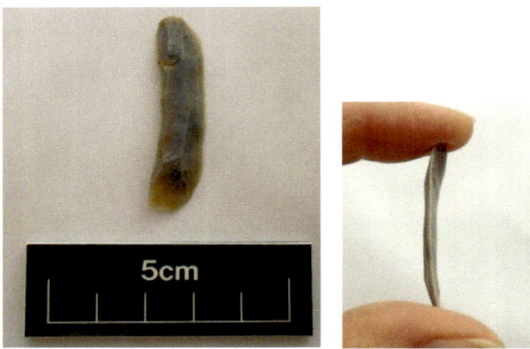

A fine late Mesolithic blade recovered from an archaeological test pit in Old Basing (photo by G. Pringle)

Big developments: the Neolithic

After the Mesolithic, around 4,000 BC the story moves on to the Neolithic, or the New Stone Age. This period sees major changes not only in the way of life of the people, but also in our landscape – some of their monuments are still visible today! It is at this time that Stonehenge, the most famous monument in the country, was begun – a monument which still excites our admiration and wonder. The most common types of evidence are as before – flint-working waste flakes and implements – but what they represent is a different way of life, because this period sees the introduction of farming and more settled occupation. In the Near East, in the so-called 'fertile crescent' of the major rivers Tigris and Euphrates, people had begun to cultivate the first grains, which meant settling in the area to harvest the sown crops. This gradually gave them more control over their food supplies, and enabled larger groups of people to live together and to develop specialist activities other than farming. At the same time, probably in Anatolia, the first steps were taken in domesticating animals. Together the ability to grow crops and herd animals made the farming package which gradually spread north and west throughout Europe. It took many centuries to reach our nearest neighbours across the Channel and during this time these people developed new ways of showing their identity and social hierarchy.

Farming did not develop naturally in this country but was introduced from the continent, which must have been a risky undertaking, given the difficulties of trussing and transporting live animals in the boats available then. But successful landfall was made both in the west – including the south west and lands bordering the Irish Sea – and via the shorter crossing from northern France and the Low Countries into southern and eastern England. There used to be discussion as to whether the idea of farming was copied by Mesolithic people seeing what was happening on the continent while on their sailing trips, but the recent advance in testing ancient DNA (aDNA) has proved the similarity between the continentals and Britain's first farmers. In some parts of Britain, the Mesolithic inhabitants continued unaffected for a time, but mostly it seems that the incoming people replaced the existing population, as Mesolithic aDNA – rare anyway – does not survive long into the Neolithic. The spread of farming was very gradual as land had to be cleared of vegetation to make fields (probably small plots) by felling trees and burning the undergrowth. The vagaries of climate and the variable fertility of soil meant that not all the initial settlements were permanent.

Burial customs

One of the features which unites all humankind is the sorrow and grief when a loved member of the family or group dies, frequently expressed in a funeral ceremony and/or a memorial of some kind. They can survive in the archaeological record better than the remains of everyday life, and because offerings were often buried with the departed, give valuable information about the people who made and used them. In some parts of Britain the early Neolithic people raised monuments called long barrows over their dead; many can still be seen and some can be recognised on aerial photographs. There are usually several burials in a long barrow, but clearly not every person could be accommodated. It has been suggested that the important members of the group, perhaps the 'founding fathers' who established and led their settlement, were honoured in this way. A long barrow is a long, tapering mound with side ditches. A great deal of work was put into its construction; at the broader end of the oval the dead were laid in a sort of shelter of timber or, in the western counties, of stone. This was followed, sometimes after subsequent burials, by the construction of the mound over them by piling earth from ditches on either side, and in some areas, a cairn of stone. This would have involved all the people of the settlement. At the broad end, there was often a façade of stone or timber, in front of which the mourning and commemorative rituals would have taken place. There are many variations on this basic arrangement and the practice of building long barrows was introduced from the continent. Recent work on their dating has demonstrated that they were built over a limited timeframe, which supports the theory that they were foundational monuments, stamping ownership on tracts of land.

The distribution of long barrows in Hampshire shows very few in the north of the county which suggests that this area was not settled early by the incomers. This interpretation is backed by the fact that another early type of monument, causewayed enclosures, is also not found in this part of the county. These enclosures surrounded by interrupted ditches (hence the name) were some of the first meeting spaces for the wider community and required a considerable amount of time and effort to construct. It is thought they were for exchanging news, trading goods and stock, celebrating marriages and so on – there is certainly evidence for feasting with deposits of animal bone in the ditches. There are many famous examples which can still be seen (Robin Hood's Ball and Windmill Hill in Wiltshire) but some are discovered by accident such as during gravel working in the Thames Valley for example, and it is always possible that one might still be recognised in our area.

Local evidence

But for now, the evidence we have in Old Basing is of the domestic variety - flint and stone tools in the main, with the already familiar site at Wellocks Hill again providing many examples. The wide spread of finds in this area, from the waterside at the bottom of the valley, up the surrounding slopes of Wellocks and Ructstalls Hills, towards Crabtree Plantation, suggest that this might be a settlement site rather than just a casual hunting venue. The flints from this period are quite distinct from those of earlier times. The flint axes are more recognisably axe-shaped in both their chipped form and in their polished state.

*Polished flint axe from Wellocks Hill with modern handle
(photo by B. Large, courtesy of Hampshire Cultural Trust)*

Polishing – the grinding of the flint with sand and water on a hard surface to give a smooth tool which would have been more efficient in use – became widespread at this time, although it is occasionally found on some Mesolithic implements. As well as axes made of flint, other hard rocks found in the more mountainous parts of Britain were selected, using the polishing technique to reach the required shape. The results can be quite beautiful, and sometimes axes are found in very deliberate positions, such as the one found beside the Sweet Track in the Somerset Levels. This axe, made of jadeite, a rock found in Austria, was in pristine unused condition, an obviously precious object which had travelled a long way. It was deliberately deposited below the water crossed by the timber track which enabled people to travel from one island in the marsh to another.

It is always risky imputing motives to people in the past, but it is hard to avoid the conclusion that this was an offering of importance perhaps to ensure the successful use of this track – the survival of which, due to the waterlogged conditions of the Somerset Levels, is remarkable in itself, especially as this track has been securely dated to 3807-6 BC. The construction of this track, with posts driven into the ground to support cross members, bridging the difficult terrain, was very sophisticated but practical. The deposit of this beautiful axe illustrates two very important facts about these Neolithic people: their ability to obtain materials from outside their local area and to transport them over great distances, and also their non-utilitarian values and way of looking at their world. The word 'ritual' can be over used, but this kind of deposit and communal activity had very important significance to them. It is further illustrated in their building monuments with no obvious practical use, like the various circular monuments with stone or timber posts, long decayed but recognised through their postholes, which must have had a social or religious significance we can only guess at.

Although it must have been difficult to establish farming settlements when they first arrived, these pioneers were eventually successful in obtaining a degree of control over and certainly an intimate knowledge of the land. It was found that useful axes could be made from certain hard rocks in Cornwall, Wales, Ireland, Scotland and the Lake District, all areas where flint does not occur naturally. In the Lake District the actual rock exposures where the rock was obtained have been discovered; they are often in very inaccessible places, such as at Langdale Pike, suggesting that the mining of the chosen rock was a special activity in itself and that those axes would have been highly prized. They have been found widely distributed in England through an efficient system of 'trade' and exchange both by sea and land, and probably given as gifts, bride prices and rewards as well as ritually deposited. The imperishable axes survive. It can only be imagined what other items were transported about the country in this way, and certainly knowledge and ideas would have been shared.

There may not be an important ritual site in Old Basing, but there is an axe from Wellocks Hill made from non-local stone, so the people living there were part of this wider network of communications. The quantity of finds found by Willis and Ellaway in one recorded instance from Wellocks Hill – 14 arrowheads, 16 polished axes, 42 chipped axes, 325 scrapers, 132 fabricators, 20 borers (borers and fabricators probably being leather working tools) and 90 other fragments (see p.17 and Ellaway & Willis, 1920) – testify to activity over a period, and there are further finds from both Crabtree Plantation and Ructstalls Hill.

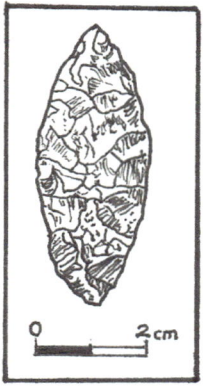

A selection of Neolithic flints from Wellocks Hill (photo by B. Large, courtesy of Hampshire Cultural Trust) and a leaf-shaped arrowhead (drawn by A. Turton)

The most characteristic arrowhead is leaf-shaped, which is a simple yet effective form. Isolated finds of these perhaps result from unsuccessful hunting, such as one found in a later feature during work to build the Infant School. An isolated chipped axe was also found by chance in a field adjacent to Pyott's Hill, indicating activity away from the chalkland, perhaps foraging for wood.

Pots and pits

Another most important introduction made by Neolithic people was pottery. The discovery, probably accidental, that heating clay gave firm, usable and waterproof containers, was made far away in the Fertile Crescent, and different styles of pottery were made by different groups as they moved across Europe. Pottery is a most valuable tool for archaeologists because it is often hard enough to survive in the ground and also because it changes in form so frequently, so that even small broken fragments can be used to identify and date the group who made it. Pots can be distinguished by their form, composition and particularly by their decoration. On these early pots this was achieved with fingertips or fingernails, or by impressing twine (often giving little impressions referred to as maggots!), twigs or even tiny bird bones into the clay while still wet, to make a pattern (see p.19). It illustrates the fundamental creative urge to adorn what is being made and gives a direct link with the potter expressing his or her choice of pattern or perhaps group identifying marks. The use of bird bones was discovered by experimenting with potential items by Dorothy Liddell, who was born in Sherfield, when she was working on the excavation of the Windmill Hill causewayed enclosure in Wiltshire in the 1920s. The impressions she made can still be seen alongside identical marks in Neolithic pottery in the museum at Avebury.

This earliest pottery was probably baked in a bonfire, hidden in the ash. Our ancestors learned early on to mix sand, ground up flint, grog (broken pot fragments), shell or even bits of grass with the clay to prevent it from shattering when it was fired. When the air was kept away from the pots, the colour would be black, grey or brown; if air was present, the iron in the clay would oxidise and the vessels would be red or brown. Pottery from so long ago does not survive well in topsoil, where it is subject to the effects of ploughing and erosion, but where there are features such as pits and postholes cut into the ground, it is more likely to survive. In 2018, there was an excavation (unpublished) by Archaeology South-East at a site previously known as Larch Plantation and close to Crabtree Plantation (see map on p.25, no.4). This was part of a planning application to build a service facility (from now on referred to as MSA) for the M3, which ultimately did not proceed. It did however result in the only examples of Neolithic pottery from the parish – fragments of a type with 'maggots', part of a bowl which had finer decoration on the rim, and other sherds with bird bone impressions. They were found in pits which also yielded pieces of antler, a very useful material throughout prehistory, being workable but hard. Antler was made into points, needles and other tools, while in the Neolithic the main branch of the antler was used as a pick for prising out the chalk subsoil when digging ditches or pits. These pits at the MSA site contained domestic rubbish and indicate that this is one of the places on the valley slope where these Neolithic people might have lived.

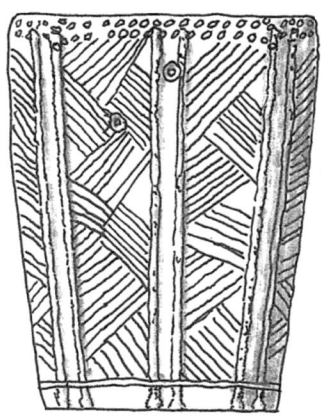
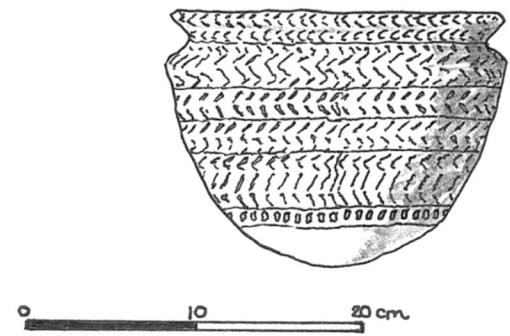

*Examples of Neolithic pottery
(redrawn by A. Turton from Annable & Simpson, 1964)*

Only just outside the parish, at the recent housing development at Merton Rise, Popley, excavations by Wessex Archaeology prior to construction work uncovered evidence of occupation from several periods, starting with the Neolithic (Wright, Powell & Barclay, 2009). The earliest definite evidence was two pottery sherds, redeposited in a tree-throw hollow, made of flint-tempered ware and decorated with twisted cord in a herringbone design. Several pits were excavated containing settlement refuse – worked flints, burnt flint, animal bone, charred hazelnut shells, charcoal, and pottery from the Late Neolithic in a style first identified in Orkney which was adopted and used across the country but is uncommon in this area. There were several different fabrics where the raw clay was mixed with a variety of tempers. Also several decorative techniques were used – fingernail impressions and shallow grooves dividing the pot into panels, and incised lines of all-over herringbone design. Base and wall fragments indicating jars and bowls were found which would have been used for cooking or storage. The decoration on some of the pottery suggests the woven pattern of baskets (see p.19). This skill is very ancient and was also used to weave (as it still is) hazel rods into fence panels which were also important in construction. At Butser Ancient Farm, there is an unfinished structure which demonstrates this technique in use for both wall and roof before daub and thatch covered them.

Partly built house at Butser Ancient Farm showing the techniques for walls and roofs (photo by P. Potter, courtesy of Butser Ancient Farm)

The professional excavations at the Merton Rise site have been important in discovering more about local archaeology because they revealed large areas and were able to explore thoroughly any evidence which remained; even a few flints and potsherds add to the picture! If the opportunity arises to do further work at Wellocks Hill, it would certainly provide more detail about this rich and extensive site, which remains our best evidence for occupation over a substantial part of the early prehistoric period. The nearest activity recently has been the evaluation work undertaken for the MSA by Archaeology South-East, which did not progress to full excavation because the facility was not built, so the evidence recovered is far from complete.

Newcomers: the 'Beaker people'

Even so, this site has provided information about the next change in the archaeological story of the parish – the arrival of the 'Beaker people'. We now know from ancient DNA analysis that between 2400 – 2300 BC groups of people entered Britain and Ireland who originated in the Steppe regions of northern Europe. They are visible archaeologically mainly through their method of burial, and an inhumation, the first deliberate burial so far discovered, was found in a pit with a beaker pot. These recognisable vessels, called after their distinctive shape, gave their name to the incomers, the 'Beaker people'.

A complete Beaker, 17cm high and 13cm diameter, from Brown Candover (photo by B. Large, courtesy of Hampshire Cultural Trust)

They are found with individual burials laid in the foetal position in a pit, sometimes under a round mound of earth - no longer surviving in this case. The best examples are almost always from these funerary locations as more domestic vessels are less fine and decorative. There are different styles of beaker decoration, the earliest being an 'all-over-cord' design which changes through time to bands of decoration with chevrons and triangles, often produced by impressing a bone comb, sometimes with white filler in the holes to contrast with the reddish colour of the pottery. The incomplete beaker from the MSA site was a globular S-shaped vessel with horizontal comb or whipped cord impressions on the neck and incised lines and chevrons on the shoulder. Only the lower half of the flexed skeleton was recovered in the evaluation trench, but the position is fully recorded should there be an opportunity for further excavation in the future. The Beaker people had learnt how to make finer, harder pottery by controlling the temperature of the firing, which was probably still taking place in bonfire kilns. This better control of fire was also shown in other new skills – smelting copper and working gold.

First metals

Evidence for these new skills is often found on Chalcolithic (Copper Age) sites where copper and copper alloy working was introduced by the newcomers from the continent. The main forms are flat copper axes which often occur as stray finds, but the majority of finds come from burial contexts. Many of the richest burials, which include copper daggers and gold objects such as adornments, are found in southern Britain, with a number being found in close vicinity to Stonehenge. Unsurprisingly, the Beaker people continued to value this splendid monument, and a degree of architectural rearrangement occurred through into the Early Bronze Age. The desire for metals, especially copper and tin, opened up new exchange networks and copper mines dating from the late third millennium BC can be found at Great Orme, North Wales and Ross Island, south-west Ireland.

Evidence for settlement from the late third millennium BC is scarce, but their characteristic burials have been found throughout this country and Europe. Objects of copper and especially gold are very rare indeed but they continued to use flint for everyday equipment, and their barbed and tanged arrowheads, illustrating an efficiency in archery, are the most recognisable of their flint tools. The illustration on p.23 shows the changes in arrowhead from a tiny flint point

(Mesolithic), leaf shaped (Neolithic) and in the centre, barbed and tanged – the tangs make the arrowhead much harder to dislodge.

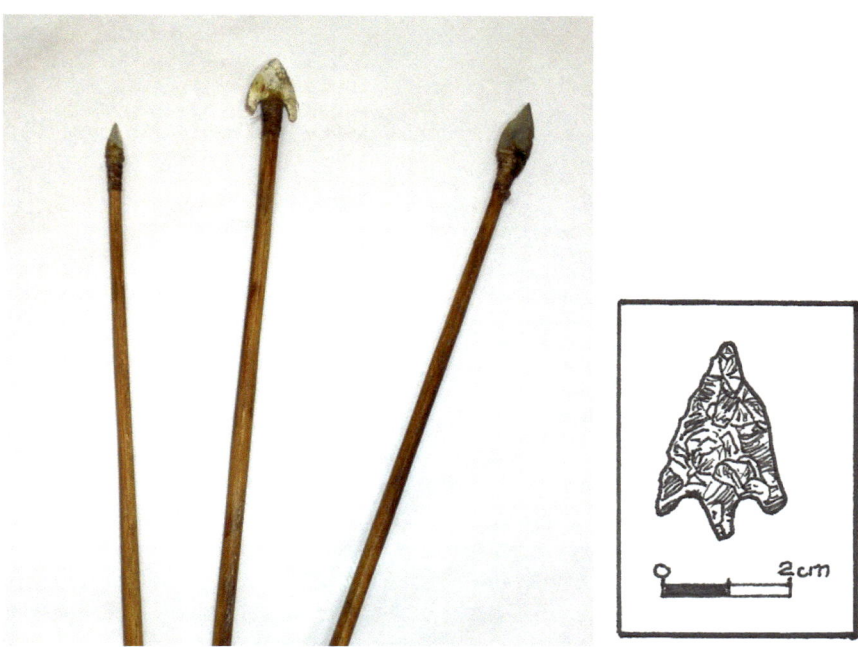

Arrowheads with modern mounts, from the left: Mesolithic, barbed and tanged and leaf-shaped (photo by B. Large, courtesy of Hampshire Cultural Trust) and a detailed drawing of a barbed and tanged arrowhead (by A. Turton)

Many older archaeological textbooks discuss whether beakers arrived in this country with people or whether it was a fashion – perhaps a religion – observed by seafarers and tradesmen crossing the Channel and adopted by people living here. However, scientific progress has resulted in firm evidence that people were indeed coming to these shores in some numbers. This evidence has been obtained through sampling aDNA already referred to in the earlier discussion of population changes. It does not routinely survive in ancient skeletons – the soil conditions have to be favourable for bone to survive at all – but a major programme of sampling of particularly dense bones in well preserved burials has resulted in uncontaminated material giving good results. It now seems likely, through comparison with later samples, that Beaker DNA gradually came to constitute at least half the DNA of Bronze Age people through settlement and intermarriage with the existing inhabitants.

The Age of Bronze

The Beaker people, with their extensive connections to the continent, were able to take advantage of further improvements in the working of metal as it progressed from copper to a copper alloy (bronze) with the addition of tin, to produce a much harder more serviceable metal. Bronze was far more suitable for edge tools and weapons. The first Bronze axes were very similar in shape to the copper flat axes, but gradually during the Bronze Age the blade edge became extended and new designs for more efficient implements were introduced. Copper and bronze daggers now developed into a whole range of equipment such as pins, razors, and jewellery as well as tools, and indicated changes in fashion including in personal appearance. Tin is a much rarer metal than copper but does occur in Cornwall and was widely traded. Metal finds of any kind are rarely found because they were highly prized and not casually disposed of, and when broken could be melted down to make new items. Substantial numbers of bronze objects are infrequently found in hoards, but bronze items are consistently buried with the important members of a community, who could be sent into the next world with offerings which mirrored their status in life. Sadly, no such rich burials have yet been found in the parish, but the people buried here were part of a group who had extensive contacts and entirely changed the complexion of British prehistory.

Further burials

Bronze Age people continued the tradition of individual burial for some under a mound of earth dug from a surrounding ditch, commonly called barrows, and these are widely found throughout the British Isles and further afield. There are examples of these in Old Basing but, after centuries of ploughing, they have not survived as earthworks and are recognised as ring ditches on aerial photographs. There is a group of three (see map on p.25) near the south-west edge of the parish on the east-facing slope of the Loddon tributary valley already referred to as a focus of settlement, but they have not been excavated. It is likely that the builders lived within sight of these barrows.

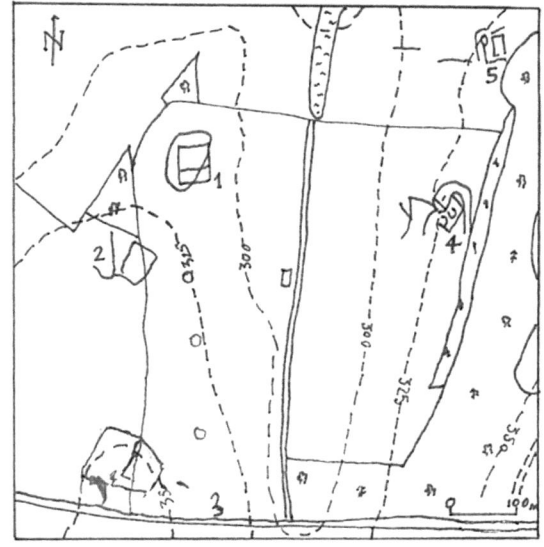

1. Ructstalls Hill
2. Common Plantation
3. Home Farm
4. Larch Plantation (MSA)
5. Oaken Plantation
O = Ring ditches

Location of sites visible on an aerial photograph of the area between Black Dam and the Tunworth road (redrawn by S. Oliver from Oliver & Applin, 1978)

Another group further north on the south facing slope above the Loddon river was identified prior to house-building at Cowdery's Down and was excavated by the County Museum Service in 1978-81 before construction began (Millett & James, 1983). This was a complex, multi-period site but the Bronze Age evidence was exciting as it uncovered the first definite evidence for the homes of these people in the Middle to Late Bronze Age. Earlier than this phase however, three ring ditches exposed after the removal of the topsoil were identified as the remains of round barrows (see p.27) and one of them still contained a burial – probably not the primary burial which no doubt would have been central and lost through the erosion of topsoil – but a secondary one placed in the barrow ditch fill consisting of eroded earth from the mound. It was the crouched burial of an adult female aged between 30 and 40, laid facing the centre of the ring, and she was accompanied by a flint knife at her waist and, more distinctively, by three adornments – a toggle made of jet and two pestle-shaped pendants made of shale (see p.26). They were found beneath her neck and she was probably wearing them when she was laid to rest. Neither shale nor jet (the latter only found in the

Whitby area) are local, and must have reached Old Basing through 'trade' – the exchange of valued items – and testify to the importance of this lady to her community. The pendant beads were perforated in a V-shape characteristic of the Beaker people and their Early Bronze Age successors, and can be closely paralleled by finds from a burial on Salisbury Plain (see Annable & Simpson, 1964).

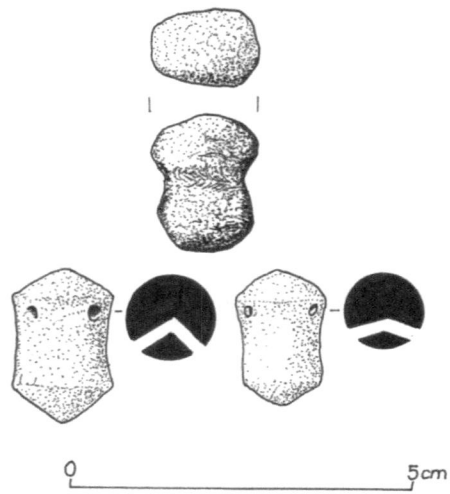

*Beads from the barrow burial at Cowdery's Down
(redrawn by A. Turton from Millett & James, 1983)*

There was also early pottery from a later level in this ditch. Rather a coarse plainware, it is frequently associated with urned cremation burials often inserted into barrow mounds. At Cowdery's Down, fragments of five different pots found their way into the ditch when the barrow mound was ploughed away, with any human remains dispersed. One of the other barrow ditches almost cut the ditch of the third, suggesting that they were not constructed at the same time, so the area continued to be favoured for a certain period as a burial site, perhaps for a family or important members of the community (there must have been lots of unaccompanied deposits of bones or ashes put into the ground which have left no trace). Cremation as a burial technique has been recognised from the Neolithic period.

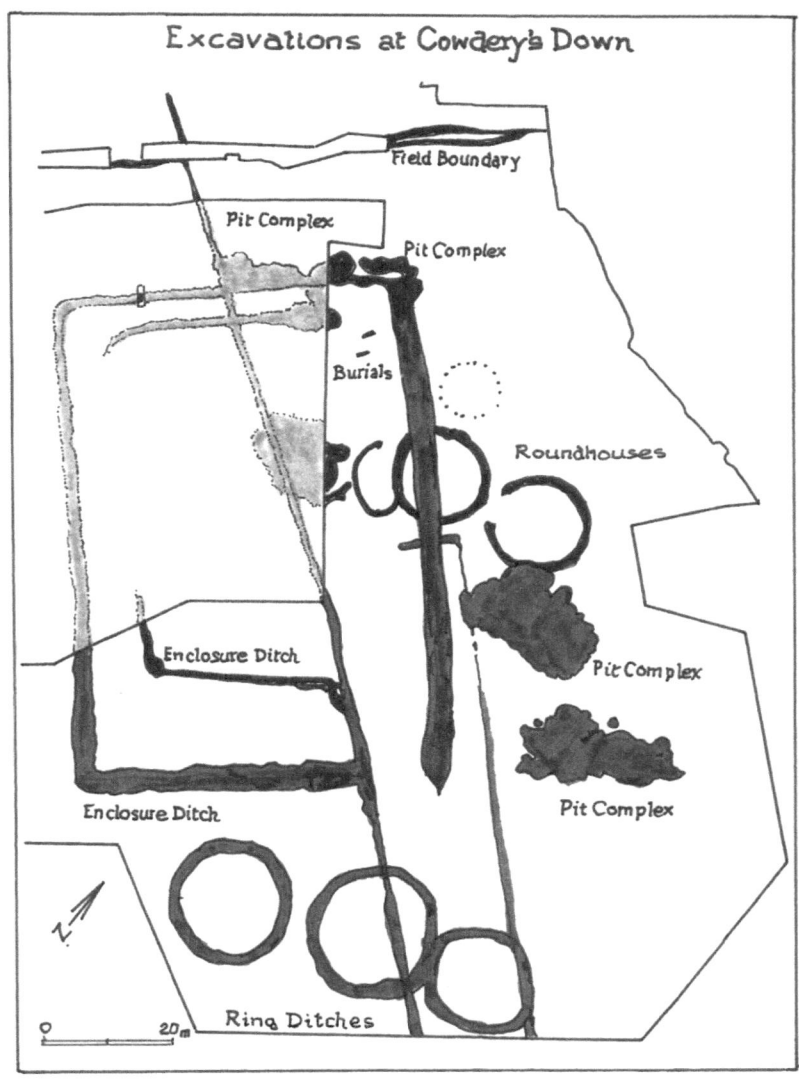

Plan showing the Early Bronze Age ring ditches, the Late Bronze Age roundhouses and pit complexes, and the Late Iron Age and Early Roman enclosure ditches; (light shading = aerial photo evidence, unexcavated) (redrawn by A. Turton from Millett & James, 1983)

Another such site within the parish, a little later in date, and excavated by the County Museum Service (Millett & Schadla-Hall, 1991) was found in 1980 when development and road building were happening at Daneshill, Chineham, and pottery was discovered in the difficult clay subsoils of the Reading Beds at the top of the hill. The cemetery was not surrounded by an enclosure ditch and the effects of ploughing erosion were considerable. There were 13 or 14 depositions (one double) found with pottery sherds tempered with ground flint and hand-smoothed. Some pieces were rim sherds, implying that the pot was placed upside-down over the ashes like a miniature cairn, and some burials were interred with just sherds rather than complete pots. No other grave goods were recovered. Two of the pots were decorated with an applied clay strip impressed with finger prints. Not all the ashes could be categorised, but those that could were identified as adults, sub adults, children and babies, so a full cross section of the community was present. Two radiocarbon dates were obtained giving a confident range of between 1600-1400 BC.

A restored burial urn from Dummer (Stevens, 1889), similar to those found at Daneshill (photo by B. Large, courtesy of Hampshire Cultural Trust)

The first recognisable houses!

Returning to Cowdery's Down, just north of the three barrow ditches was a further series of three round ditches, but the profile and filling of these has caused them to be interpreted as structural, probably to take the wall supports. One of these ring ditches was not a complete circle, but looked like an annexe to its neighbour – a situation paralleled on other sites as a storeroom, workshop or animal shelter. The entrance to the third faces the complete circle, which perhaps suggests they were not in use at the same time (see p.27). In addition there was a circle of 17 postholes with two outliers to the south-east, interpreted as a post-built roundhouse with a porched entrance facing south-east, towards the morning light. A circular house built around timber posts is a form very commonly found from the Mid/Late Bronze Age through the Iron Age and into the Roman period (see p.30). The walls were finished with a mud/clay/dung/straw mix daubed onto the wattle between the posts which dried to give a weather-proof finish; it is referred to as 'daub', and the baked evidence of this technique survives from many sites where buildings have burnt down. The practice survived into historic times in areas where there was no suitable building stone and until bricks became easily available. The little group of structures at Cowdery's Down provides the evidence for the first recognisable homes in the village! By this time, the countryside would have become more fully utilised, with areas of cultivation, pasture and woodland, with lanes and route-ways to connect neighbouring farmsteads.

The erosion of the topsoil above the Cowdery's Down houses meant there was no surviving occupation surface or dating evidence, but they were associated with groups of pits which did contain domestic debris – pottery, burnt daub, some animal bone from food residue, and the carbonised seeds of wheat and oats. The pits would have originally been dug to extract the chalk, used in making daub to apply to the walls, and for marling fields on the clay subsoil to the north. They would then have been filled with what was conveniently around and the biggest collection of Late Bronze Age pottery from the parish was recovered from these intercutting pits. This included coarse ware jars and bowls, hand-made from local clays, and many decorated with finger-tipping. All this evidence suggests a small farming community growing crops and tending animals but which also had access to metal, as a small fragment of copper alloy typical of the Late Bronze Age was found. The site was probably occupied for many years. Their activities spread west along the side of the valley and a few sherds of pottery and some flints were found during trial trenching prior to house building along Basing Road, a site referred to as Swing Swang Lane (excavated by Wessex Archaeology in October 2020 and as yet unpublished).

A reconstruction of a Bronze Age hut at Butser Ancient Farm, showing two possible walling techniques, using tamped earth on the left and daub on the right (photo by P. Potter, courtesy of Butser Ancient Farm)

By the end of the Bronze Age more metal was in circulation. Further evidence of this was a stray find from Daneshill, not far away – a rare piece of a bronze ingot (Millett & Schadla-Hall, 1991), (see p.31). There was nothing found with this, which was possibly a piece lost by a trader – and no doubt the cause of much dismay! Similarly, a bronze socketed hammer, very rare, a chance find in a field across the valley not far from the river Loddon, provides further evidence of activity in the wider area (see p.31). The hammer was well used with a worn and corroded surface but is not now available to study. There were other sites in the Basingstoke area occupied during the Late Bronze Age, with evidence at the hillfort at Winklebury (Smith, 1977), also at Buckskin (Allen *et al*, 1995) and from Marnel Park (Wright, Powell & Barclay, 2009). It is probable that many sites continued to be occupied into the Iron Age. Although archaeologists label sites and finds by period, the transition from one to another was probably very gradual.

*Piece of bronze ingot from Daneshill
(photo by B. Large, courtesy of Hampshire Cultural Trust)*

Bronze socketed hammer (PAS HAMP-1F3730)

Into the Iron Age

Some of the local evidence for Early and Middle Iron Age occupation came from Ructstalls Hill (Oliver & Applin, 1978), now the Black Dam estate, which was in the parish until recent boundary changes. This site, due to be developed for housing, was one of the reasons for the founding of the Basingstoke Archaeological Society back in 1971 when the local Willis Museum had moved its headquarters to Winchester as part of the expanding County Museum Service. As at Cowdery's Down, this site was first identified on aerial photographs, and so presented the opportunity to record and study it more fully to help interpret similar sites which could only be sampled such as those at Oakridge in Basingstoke (Oliver *et al*, 1992). But the site could not be completely excavated, as another rescue site in Basingstoke claimed the volunteer diggers! The situation of Ructstalls Hill, on the east facing slope of the now familiar tributary valley (see p.2), is interesting because the evidence of aerial photos shows that there are several other sites nearby (see map on p.25).

On the opposite side of the valley there is another group of enclosure ditches at the MSA site, where the Beaker burial as well as dating evidence similar to Ructstalls was found. There is Iron Age material from Wellocks Hill where pits containing pottery, animal bone and some small finds were visible in the chalk quarry face and recovered in the 1950s, now in the Willis Museum (HER 20474).

Middle/Late Iron Age finds, including a spindle whorl, from Wellocks Hill (photo by B. Large, courtesy of Hampshire Cultural Trust)

There are traces of prehistoric fields further east, all that remain of a probably extensive field system, and nearby, just south of the M3 at Huish, is another complex site (HER 36044) known from an aerial photo and field-walking material found by Mr Willis and his colleagues. The classic Early Iron Age date of the pottery (HER 20436) backs up the work on enclosure types, which dates the curvilinear shapes and drove-ways to this period (Pringle, 2014).

Early Iron Age pottery with finger-tipped rims from Huish (photo by B. Large, courtesy of Hampshire Cultural Trust)

There was another group of sites at the top of Pyotts Hill, running along the northern edge of the Loddon Valley towards Chineham. These sites are important as they show that there was also settlement on the clay and gravel soils in the north of the parish, only discovered recently through construction work. Iron Age finds were discovered during work at Datronech, close to Daneshill House (HER 20379); further material came from the road scrape close to where the Bronze Age cremation cemetery was excavated, and more recently, prior to building at Great Binfields Copse, now in Chineham parish (HER 53215). Part of this site revealed three gullies which probably surrounded three roundhouses, also some postholes, pits with dateable pottery and stretches of ditch. One pit also contained iron slag, implying ironworking on site. The greater availability of sources of iron ore, here low grade iron pan formed by the leaching of iron salts in the clay, made it possible for farming sites to have access to better quality tools and equipment, such as iron nails for construction and efficient iron knives and edge tools.

Looking at the distribution map of these sites, we can see parts of our parish were well populated with evenly spaced farms. We do not know how many of them were occupied at the same time, nor what the relationship between them was, or the precise role of the larger site at Winklebury. This hillfort was occupied during the Early and Middle Iron Age (Smith, 1977) and it is likely that it acted as the centre for trade of items not available locally such as salt, for gatherings for religious or social events and if necessary, defence. It must have taken a local leader of some kind to organise the construction of the considerable banks and ditches there!

*A group of reconstructed Iron Age houses at Butser Ancient Farm
(photo by P. Potter, courtesy of Butser Ancient Farm)*

Iron Age lifestyle

Returning to Ructstalls Hill, the evidence there gives a picture of a settlement enclosed within a ditch (presumably accompanied by a bank) defining the area of activity, the family's dwellings, belongings, livestock and storage areas. There is evidence, particularly from the fill of the pits, postholes and ditches, for everyday life such as food residue; animal bones from cattle, sheep and goats; some traces of metal working (slag) and iron objects (nails and a broken blade); textile working (spindle whorls and loom weights), and the pottery so useful in charting the changes over time in fashion and prosperity. The survival of some of these items – such as the spindle whorls (see the spindle whorl found at Wellocks Hill on p.32), polished and decorated bone knife handles, daub from the house walls, a sarsen grindstone pebble with its rubbing stone, a whetstone for sharpening iron blades – all bring these people and their daily lives vividly to mind.

Planning and excavation at Ructstalls Hill in 1972-3 (photo by R. Applin)

*Sarsen grindstone from a pit, Ructstalls Hill
(photo by B. Large, courtesy of Hampshire Cultural Trust)*

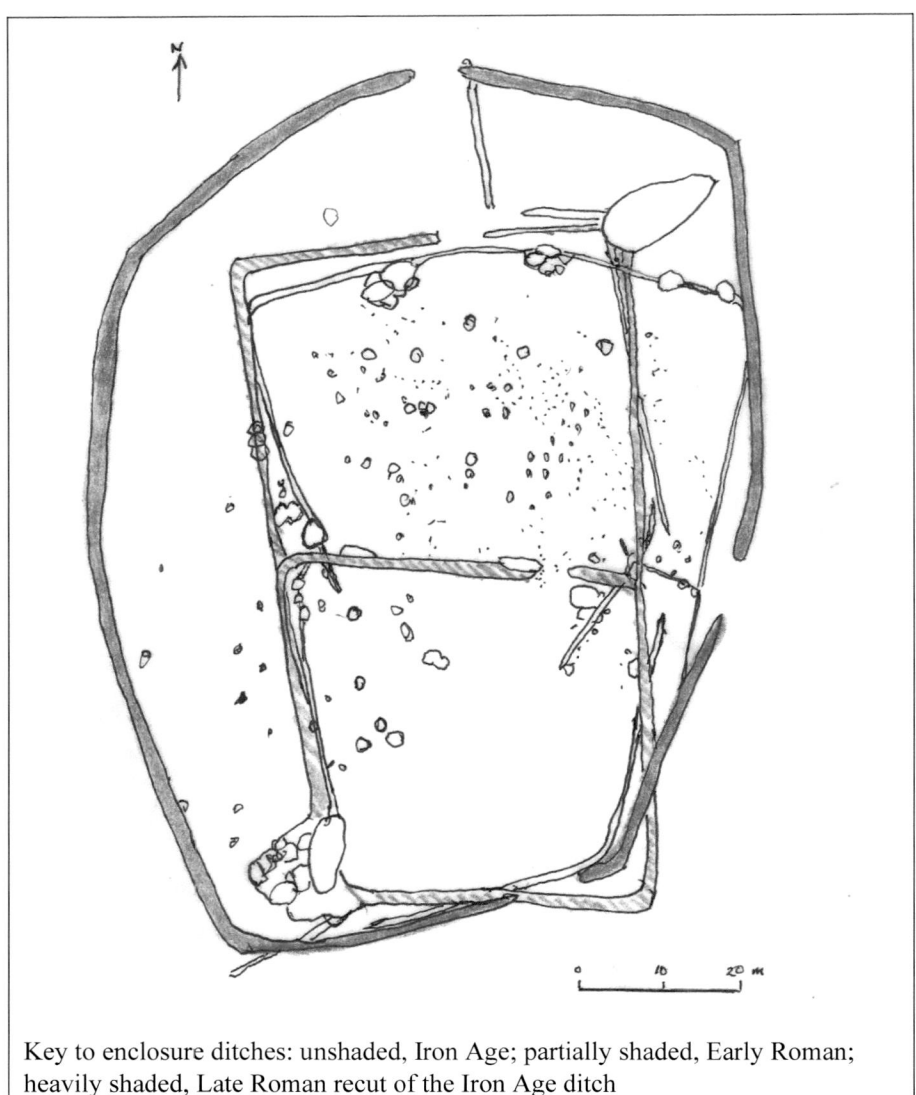

Key to enclosure ditches: unshaded, Iron Age; partially shaded, Early Roman; heavily shaded, Late Roman recut of the Iron Age ditch

Plan of Ructstalls Hill (redrawn by M. Oliver from Oliver & Applin, 1978)

The ground surface of this site has been continuously farmed for centuries, with the resulting loss of topsoil, so the shallower structures were difficult to identify fully, but there were enough postholes to indicate the position of some of their homes. Some of the postholes were very substantial, and contained big flint packing stones to support the large timber posts. It is believed that they supported four-post above-ground buildings for storage, most likely the grain supplies of the community – exactly as staddle-stone granaries did for more recent farmers, keeping precious grain out of the reach of vermin and damp.

Other important crops, including seed corn, were probably stored in pits dug into the chalk. It has been proved by experiments that, contrary to expectations, grain stored in pits, properly sealed, can be kept over winter in good condition. The moisture in the chalk, and under the clay and earth sealing cap, causes the grain it comes into contact with to germinate, which uses the available oxygen and gives off carbon dioxide. This protects the rest of the contents and leads to successful germination in the spring. This briefly summarises careful experimental work at Butser Ancient Farm in Hampshire, where the Iron Age lifestyle is very well portrayed using excavated evidence to suggest possible interpretations. The economy was one of mixed farming – the cultivation of emmer (an early variety of wheat), bearded barley and some pulses, combined with the rearing of animals, mostly sheep, (from the skeletal evidence, a small breed similar to Soay sheep), also goats, a few pony-sized horses and pigs. There were also cattle, again much smaller than modern stock. They provided milk, meat, leather, sinews and traction for ploughing.

At Butser Ancient Farm, it is possible also to see reconstructions of roundhouses (see page 34) and other features of Iron Age life based on excavated evidence from named sites. Some of these houses are surprisingly spacious, and the arrangements within, of central hearths, sleeping and working areas, enable visitors and students to visualise life at that time. Although seemingly simple, the way of life was quite complex, with the management of woodlands to supply timber for all the different uses (large posts for structures, hazel rods for fencing and walls, fuel for hearths and furnaces); the sourcing of raw materials such as metal ore, and smelting and smithing the ore into tools and equipment; the organisation of the farming year for crops and animals; the manufacture of cloth and making of clothes; tanning; brewing; and trading surplus to obtain what could not be produced on the settlement, such as salt. It seems likely that, over time, not all settlements concentrated on all these activities, such as ironworking. Sites with a better availability of raw materials would probably have specialised in tools to trade for other items from other sites.

Pits

Returning to pits, the filling of those at Ructstalls Hill, once they had fulfilled their original function, could be very informative. Sometimes they were allowed to silt up naturally, but sometimes they were filled quickly, which can be seen from the stratigraphy. One from the early occupation had the waste of an iron smelting episode dumped in the pit, as shown below.

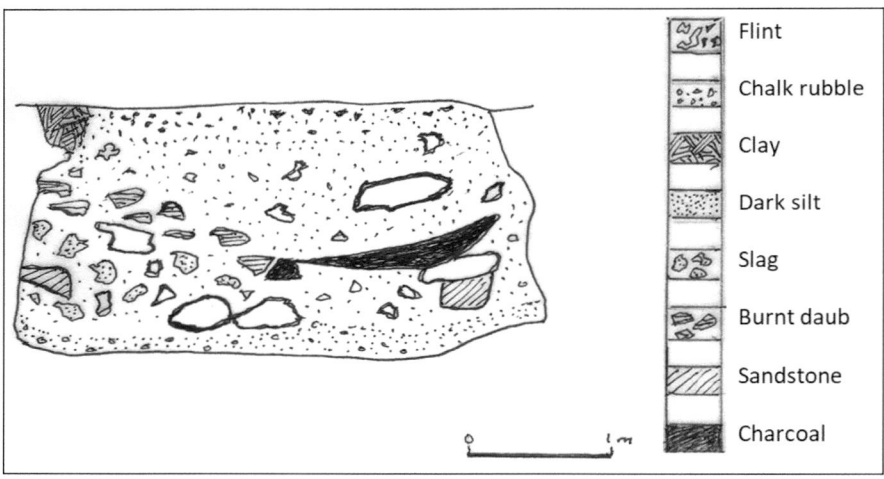

Section through a pit fill, including slag, charcoal and burnt daub, Ructstalls Hill (redrawn by M. Oliver from Oliver & Applin, 1978)

Occasionally there was an object at the bottom of the pit – a pot or an animal skull for example – which looked as if it were deliberately placed. This could be interpreted as a closure ritual in thanks for the useful purpose the pit had fulfilled. It is something which is not infrequently found on sites of this date.

Literary sources from the Roman period indicate that the pre-Roman inhabitants of Britain had a rich spiritual life. Unlike earlier times, until the Late Iron Age there is much less evidence for the treatment of the dead. It has been suggested that bodies could have been exposed to the elements or consigned to water.

The earliest pottery, as at Cowdery's Down, consisted mainly of jars, some with fingertip decoration. There is much more pottery and evidence of every kind from the Middle Iron Age, when most of the pits were dug. There are more vessel types and different fabrics and decoration, for storage, cooking and table use. One type, a small cylindrical pot, is known as a saucepan pot (from the shape, without a handle), and these were frequently burnished (polished with a piece of bone or wood before firing) to a pleasing finish. Often they were decorated with a blunt tool to make grooves and lines. These, and small globular bowls, were probably used for drinking. These forms were common throughout the area, with the styles of decoration giving an indication of possible tribal affiliation. They remained popular over a long period of time, as did the larger bowls and jars used for cooking and storage. The same kind of pottery was also found in the enclosure ditches at Cowdery's Down (Millett & James, 1983) and at Winklebury hillfort (Smith, 1977).

A complete saucepan pot from Winklebury hillfort
(photo by B. Large, courtesy of Hampshire Cultural Trust)

Contact with Rome

The transition from Bronze Age to Iron Age seems to have been characterised by development and improvements through the greater availability of resources such as iron, and traded items such as salt, but big changes also happened towards the end of the Iron Age, probably through contact with the wider world and especially the influence of Rome. There is written evidence of the influx of people from northern Gaul under their king, Commius, who clashed with Julius Caesar and who came to these shores and settled in Hampshire with his tribe known as the 'Atrebates'. This probably represents the wider trend of population movement at this time. Silchester was the chief settlement of the Atrebates, where there is certainly evidence for the import of wine and luxuries from the continent (Fulford, 2021). This period saw the introduction of coinage, not initially in the modern sense of everyday change, but of precious gold or silver items used to show wealth and for high status gifts. Two such gold coins, sadly of unrecorded provenance, were found somewhere 'between Odiham and Basingstoke' (HER 19685).

A typical Iron Age gold stater
(photo by B. Large, courtesy of Hampshire Cultural Trust)

There are also silver coins dated 40-50 BC found by metal detectorists in the parish, and several have been found in the Basingstoke area. One type is identified as the 'Old Basing type', as the first one found was in this parish (see p.41). With a stylised head on one side and a horse and chariot wheel on the reverse, inspired by a coin of Philip of Macedon, they are examples of 'Celtic' design. This wonderful art style is found usually on precious metal items of which we have no other local example, but it is entirely possible that items of wood or leather were decorated too, and even the walls of their houses, and maybe even their own bodies!

Old Basing type silver unit, c.50-40 BC
(copyright Chris Rudd Ltd, www.celticcoins.com)

Many of the Later Iron Age sites continue through the period between Caesar and Claudius and into the Roman period proper – Wellocks Hill, Ructstalls Hill, Cowdery's Down, MSA, Huish, Datronech at Daneshill, and a site at Basing House (Allen & Anderson, 1999), among them. There were however more sites discovered through building work in the northeast sector of the parish which seems to represent an expansion of activity off the easily cultivable chalklands into the more difficult clays; sites such as Great Binfield Copse (HER 53215), another at Daneshill (HER 32399), also one at Razor's Farm, Chineham (Sanigar & Andrews, 2020) until recently part of Old Basing parish, and another at Marnel Park in neighbouring Popley (Wright, Powell & Barclay, 2009). The proximity of the Roman road to Silchester and the route to the market for their animals and other produce will have been an important factor.

As contact with the new regime increased, pottery was traded, not made on site by every household, and a market economy with specialist production of certain items became established. In the early Roman period, the pottery was a mixture of the local well-established types, and pots made by early commercial pottery kilns from further afield producing wheel-thrown pottery. The nearest were at Alice Holt, near Farnham (Lyne & Jefferies, 1979). All the local sites have wares from this source and this recognisable pottery continued through to the end of the period with changing forms over the years. Even a single pot can be informative: an isolated piece from these kilns, dating from the late 1st/early 2nd centuries, was found in a ditch during the 2020 evaluation of the Swing Swang Lane site and is similar to the pot shown on p.45. There may have been a connection with the nearby contemporary site on Cowdery's Down, or with another Late Iron Age/Romano-British site to the west at Basing View excavated by Oxford Archaeology (Allen & Boothroyd, 2020).

The Romans

The Roman occupation from AD 43 is marked locally by the continuation of the trends already acknowledged, changes in settlement shape and sometimes style of building, and by a greater volume of traded goods due to access to a bigger market economy, resulting in a rise in the standard of living for most people. This can be seen in the greater variety of pottery types, in both cooking and table wares, which illustrates developments in cooking and eating habits, and in the different items of jewellery signalling changing fashions in costume and personal appearance (see below and p.43).

Early Roman brooches from Ructstalls Hill
(redrawn by A. Turton from Oliver & Applin, 1978)

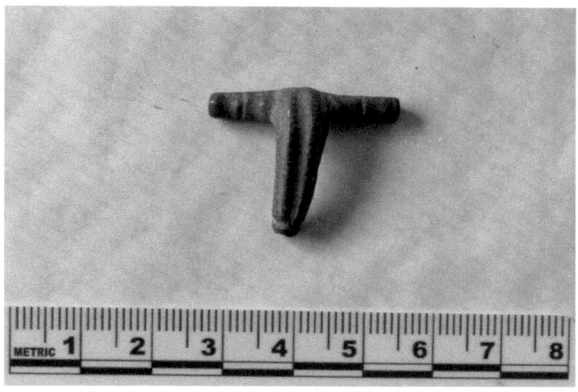

*Another style of Roman brooch, found at Wellocks Hill
(photo by B. Large, courtesy of Hampshire Cultural Trust)*

The kite-shaped enclosure ditch at Ructstalls Hill (see p.36) was replaced at this time by a rectangular enclosure which was then divided in half to give two square enclosures, both used at the same time. This trend for rectilinear enclosures can also be seen at Cowdery's Down (Millet & James, 1983), at Common Plantation (the nearest site to Ructstalls), at Daneshill (Millett & Schadla-Hall, 1991), at Razor's Farm (Sanigar & Andrews, 2020) and Basing View (Allen & Boothroyd, 2020) in the neighbourhood, and at other sites in the Basingstoke area (e.g. Viables (Millett & Russell, 1984) and Worting (Lalor, 2015)), and they were often associated with droveways. This reorganisation of land and boundaries indicates a level of activity, perhaps ownership changes and/or investment through contact with the Atrebates and/or the Roman authorities. It is likely that they were connected with stock rearing, with the nearby town of Silchester providing a ready market. There is evidence of activity from chance finds of pottery, such as at Huish near to a site clearly shown on an aerial photo which appears to be an Iron Age enclosed site but with rectangular ditches too (HER 36044). It lies close to the valley of the Lyde, a chalk stream in the east of the parish which flows north-east to join the Loddon. In the vicinity of the old Chineham brickworks near Daneshill, a considerable amount of Roman material was recovered from several workings when the brickworks were in production (HER 20382) and similarly there were Roman finds, including an early 4th century coin, from the sand pit next to the brickworks just beyond the recreation ground in the village (HER 20440). This coin is made of copper alloy, a 'follis' of the emperor Galerius Valerius Maximianus, minted in Turkey between AD 305 and 311. The emperor's head is on the obverse, but the reverse shows a 'genius', a protective personal god, holding a wreath and cornucopia (a horn of plenty), all combining to wish the emperor good fortune.

The coin found in the 19th century sandpit in Riley Lane
(photo by B. Large, courtesy of Hampshire Cultural Trust)

Further evidence includes a few potsherds found during the BAHS Dig Basing project (Pringle, 2020) and some during groundwork for the Old Basing Health Centre, together giving a 'background noise' of Roman activity in the village itself. This might be the result of past spreading of midden and manure heaps on the land to fertilise it and if so would suggest the close proximity of occupation sites.

There is considerably more evidence of Romano-British occupation in and around the site of Basing House as pottery has shown up during the excavation of the better known phases of the village's most important monument (Allen & Anderson, 1999). Work to the south of the citadel in the 1960s by the Aldermaston Archaeological Society (Combley *et al*, 1964), and further exploration of the same area in 2013 by the University of Southampton, confirmed occupation in the Late Iron Age and, as at so many sites, this continued into the Roman period. A quantity of material from early to late Roman times has been found from various parts of the site, including a variety of pottery – the big, flint-gritted storage jars, fine table ware from non-local kilns and much 'everyday' greyware mostly from the kilns at Alice Holt near Farnham.

Part-restored greyware jar from Basing House
(photo by B. Large, courtesy of Hampshire Cultural Trust)

One of the certain indicators of trade with the Roman world is imported Samian pottery – very distinctive bright red vessels, the 'best china' of the time. It was imported initially from Italy, then from Gaul and later still, from the Rhineland until it was overtaken by other fashions. It was obtainable for our local inhabitants at Basing House (Allen & Anderson, 1999), and other sites, through the markets at Silchester, and possibly through pedlar salesmen visiting the farms with their packhorses.

Samian pottery from Razor's Farm
(photo by B. Large, courtesy of Hampshire Cultural Trust)

The road

Silchester was linked to the village via the main road from Silchester to Chichester. Its course has been plotted (see p.2), and many of our Roman sites were within easy reach of the road. It is no longer visible as a monument, but it was a main artery of communication within the kingdom of the Atrebates and dates from early on in the occupation. An undated section of the 'agger', the bank on which the road was built, was found during cable laying work in 2001 (a watching brief by Thames Valley Archaeological Services (HER 51493)) close to where the road's course passes from Chineham to Old Basing. The making of the road was possibly preceded by a route-way running north west/south east, and similar long-standing routes such as the Harrow Way have been recognised for many years. Unlike the road between Silchester and Winchester, it did not continue as a major route into historic times.

A glance at the map of the settlement of Roman Britain as a whole illustrates how much of a stimulus to settlement was the proximity of a road. For our local Romano-Britons, it was their link to the central hub, where they would find amenities not available locally, such as legal or medical. It was also their chance to hear news of the wider Roman world, and to enjoy the delights of the amphitheatre and all it had to offer. One such site close to the road and benefitting from easy access to the market is Razor's Farm, excavated in 2016 by Wessex Archaeology prior to housing development (Sanigar & Andrews, 2020). There was a Late Iron Age phase, a larger early Roman enclosure, then a mid to late Roman rectangular enclosure; no structural evidence was found, but this rural settlement yielded sherds of wine amphorae, Samian bowls and fragments of glass vessels which most likely came down the road from Silchester and illustrate the rise in standard of living for ordinary Romano-Britons.

Roman vessel glass from Razor's Farm
(photo by B. Large, courtesy of Hampshire Cultural Trust)

Roman buildings

Many of the farms continued to use roundhouses of the traditional type, but what everyone associates with the Romans is a much more luxurious type of house, a villa, a substantially built structure with mosaic floors, central heating, and a bath suite, such as have been found at Chedworth, Bignor, and Sparsholt near Winchester, the latter now reconstructed at Butser Ancient Farm.

A reconstruction of a Roman villa (based on excavations at Sparsholt, Hampshire) at Butser Ancient Farm
(photo by P. Potter, courtesy of Butser Ancient Farm)

Such buildings are not found as frequently as all that, but there is a range of types which can be called villas, some are quite simple but rectangular in plan and with evidence of Roman building materials and appurtenances. One likely candidate for a villa in the parish was discovered some years ago on the north bank of the Loddon near the decoy pond on land east of Lodge Farm. The recorded finds in the museum include *'tegulae'* roof tiles, flue and hypocaust tiles implying a heating system, and some tesserae from a pavement floor (see p.49). Also found were fragments of Samian ware as well as Alice Holt greywares. The site has not been excavated – these are all stray finds – but they are enough for it to be included in the list of likely villas (Applebaum, 1953), and the waterside site, a short distance from the road to Silchester, in fertile farming land, provides an ideal position. As there is no threat to the site at the moment, there is no reason for it to be excavated; techniques of recording and recovery improve all the time, so it is important to leave sites for future generations.

Fragments of limestone roof tiles, clay tiles and tesserae from east of Lodge Farm (photo by B. Large, courtesy of Hampshire Cultural Trust)

It is also likely that the considerable Roman material found at Basing House during exploration of the Civil War works also amount to a substantial structure. As well as pottery, dating from the 1st to 5th centuries, and coins (mostly 4th century) the finds included building materials such as roofing, wall and flue tiles, and a possible floor surface. As there is no good building stone, except for locally available flint, it is likely that timber and wattle and daub continued to be used for the wall panels, as both before and after the Roman conquest. Again, the site, overlooking the Loddon on rising ground, is one which has been chosen and returned to over the centuries. A background scatter of potsherds exists throughout the village, and the BAHS Dig Basing project recovered another coin from The Street!

Roman pottery is better fired than most prehistoric pottery, and therefore more likely to survive the effects of agricultural activity and natural weathering. All the evidence points to a reasonable amount of activity in the parish over the 400 years or so of the Roman occupation, which for most of that time was a period of peace and stability. There were developments and changes within that time; the size of farm animals increased with selective breeding, particularly sheep and cattle, and polled remains of both species have been found. Domestic fowl were introduced by the Romans and kept for eggs, meat and feathers. Spelt wheat became the most commonly grown variety of wheat, and special corn-driers were sometimes built to assist the processing of crops, including the chitting of barley for beer. One such structure, with a stoke hole and T-shaped flue which would have been surmounted by a drying floor, was glimpsed during the groundwork for the M3 close to Common Plantation and Ructstalls Hill as it disappeared beneath the mighty road scraper! It is possible that these neighbouring sites were part of one estate and worked together. The only later Roman structure identified at Ructstalls Hill was a post-built structure built within the kite-shaped ditch, re-cut after the rectangular ditches had silted up. This modest structure could have been the stockman's house, or for storage. One fragment of window glass was found in one of the post holes, and there was a quantity of roof tiles nearby in the ditch terminals of the northern entrance so there must have been a well-roofed building somewhere close by. An indication that there was more than simply animal rearing taking place was the discovery of a pair of robust iron dividers, possibly used by a builder rather than a draughtsman and a sophisticated find in that context. An iron ox goad, also found, was a more typical rural artefact.

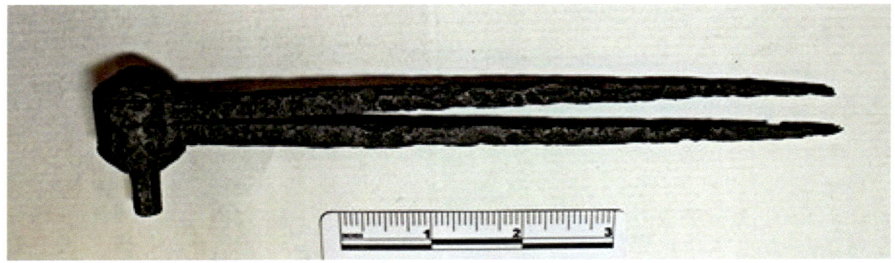

Iron dividers from Ructstalls Hill
(photo by B. Large, courtesy of Hampshire Cultural Trust)

Burials

During the Iron Age, there is little evidence of burial technique in the county, except for occasional warrior burials or inhumations in pits, until the Late Iron Age when cremation burials became more common. At Ructstalls Hill there were two cremations, contained in two Alice Holt jars of the same design, in the corner of the site in a disturbed area used for obtaining chalk. These pots were like the pot illustrated on p.45, a very common type. The Romans used both interment and cremation for their dead, with varying degrees of ceremony, and burials are frequently found. There were three baby burials in the enclosure ditches of the early Roman period, and one from the later period cut into the top of an Iron Age pit. A small section of a bronze necklace with 13 tiny, square, blue glass beads was found in the same context. Infant mortality was high – these type of burials have been found in many local sites, for instance at nearby Common Plantation and at Oaken Plantation (see map on p.25 no.5), MSA, Cowdery's Down, and at Basing View. These little members of the family were kept close to home, whereas the usual Roman way, especially in the towns and larger settlements, was to have a separate burial ground away from the centre of occupation.

However, at Daneshill where the Roman site was not completely explored, two cremation burials were found just within the enclosure ditch (Millett & Schadla-Hall, 1991). The first grave was disturbed by a JCB digger and the cremated remains lost, but the second grave was well recorded, and the remains were those of an adult female. Both burials were of a particular type recognised in the north Hampshire/Surrey borders, in which the cremations were accompanied by a large number of pots, 21 with one and 11 with the other, and both were found with many iron nails. This suggests both burial groups were contained within wooden boxes. Both dated from the mid/late 3rd century, which is somewhat later than the main tradition, (late $1^{st}/2^{nd}$ century), and the pots all came from the Alice Holt kilns. Both included a particular pedestal-based jar thought to be associated with ritual activity and often found with burials. So these two inhabitants of this modest farm were buried with considerable care and ceremony.

A further unusual burial tradition was found at Cowdery's Down. Some 100 metres east of the settlement, a double inhumation grave was found during the building work. The earlier burial was that of a young woman which had been disturbed and was reburied, disarticulated, over the feet of the second burial – that of an older woman of about 40 who was laid on her back, but whose skull was found near her knees (Grainger, 1983). Hobnails from a pair of boots or shoes, a Roman characteristic, were near the feet and suggest the body might have been buried clothed. The rite of decapitation is not uncommon. It is not something which is well understood, but it was clearly not necessarily punitive. There were loose bones in this area which was disturbed, having been used for obtaining chalk, and may explain why it was chosen as a cemetery area for the site. Two other burials, both mature males, and damaged by house footings, were found close together within the Roman enclosure. One buried face down had hobnails near his feet. The other had a severe wound to the left femur, which initially caused the excavators to think the individual might have been a Civil War casualty, as there was a 17th century camp in that location (Grainger, ibid.). Recent radio carbon dating of the wounded individual returned a Roman date (King & Cole, 2016). There must be many such burials in the village, given the amount of Roman settlement, but many will have been destroyed by agricultural activity and others are only likely to be discovered by accident.

Religion

Other than the care taken with the disposal of the dead, there is no direct evidence for religious observance during the Roman period in Old Basing. Because of written records, we know that many of the pantheon of the Graeco-Roman gods were enthusiastically adopted by the residents of Britain. They were often identified with a local deity with the same attributes, such as warrior strength, fertility, wisdom, protection in childbirth, etc. Added to the mix was emperor worship – compulsory – and for some, later in the period, Christianity. The nearest we have to a representation of a divinity in the parish is a copper alloy piece with an iron bolt and strap behind, possibly a furniture fitting, which shows the head of Oceanus (see p.53 and Bristow & Harrap, 2024). He was the deity of the ocean, which flows round the edge of the world, and closely associated with remote Britain. Identified by his seaweed moustache and dolphins in his beard, Romans saw him as the source of all life. It is an important piece of Roman art and was certainly not made locally but may well have been imported as a luxury item from Campania in Italy where there was a flourishing bronze founding industry. It looks as if the strap has been torn off its original fixing, which may have been a strong box (a Roman safe) as there are parallels at Pompeii. However the head of Oceanus was valued enough to be safely removed and kept, whether to be venerated or enjoyed for its beauty or even planned for recycling, we can never know.

The Oceanus head, now in the British Museum (Surrey County Council)

Big changes

The relatively settled period of Britain being a province of the Roman Empire came to an end during the 5th century. This was another of those times when there was large scale movement of population with people migrating west and pressing on the borders of the empire. The troops in Britain were gradually withdrawn to defend the centres of power, with the official instruction for the local leaders to take measures for their own defence. The withdrawal of soldiers meant that there was no longer an influx of money to pay them, so gradually the monetary economy wound down. Generally there were no sudden changes, and businesses no doubt continued as long as they could, but there are reports of widespread plague, and the native population seems to have declined. The threat of invading 'barbarians' from across the North Sea was already familiar to those on the coast, and the Saxon Shore forts were built to defend the east and south coasts with the support of the navy.

The Roman authorities had always recruited soldiers and sailors from their provinces to fight for them. One of the tactics was to settle tribal groups on a fixed area of land within the border in exchange for defending it. This happened in Britain, as recorded in the Anglo Saxon Chronicle, with the arrival of Hengist and Horsa and their followers in Kent at the invitation of the warlord, Vortigern. This famous document cannot be regarded as an accurate historical record but it describes the pattern of events from the mid-5th century. Other Saxon princes are also recorded, including Cerdic and Cynric in Hampshire, with the common theme that they eventually turned against their hosts and gradually took over more and more land. It was not a straightforward process and there were battles for control throughout Wessex. It must have been a very difficult time for the existing population. However, recent work on the aDNA of burials in Saxon cemeteries has shown that people did eventually intermarry and settle down, adopting the new way of life, artefacts and homes. The movement of people from the continent to Britain was repeated countless times throughout history and indeed into modern times. Each group brought something to the cultural development of the country and added to the genetic mix of the population.

Saxon Basing

It is from this period that a site in Old Basing featured in the national archaeological press with a major contribution! During the excavations at Cowdery's Down (already referred to), the post holes initially expected to be Civil War defences for the Parliamentary battery, turned out to be the support posts for Saxon halls. The important feature was the quality of preservation of the evidence – in some cases it was possible to discern the shape of the posts, planks and stakes and work out how the buildings were constructed. The settlement was on the crest of the slope, slightly uphill from the earlier archaeology, and formed three phases of build, each increasing in size and complexity.

The earliest, erected in the 6th century, was a group of three rectangular halls, with opposing doors on the longer sides and one had an annexe. They were set within two fenced enclosures (it was fence posts which first gave the clue about the settlement's existence). At least one of the buildings was burned down and the settlement was quickly rebuilt in the same location, three halls within enclosures.

The replacement buildings were structurally more complex, with accurately cut opposing timbers within each posthole which would have supported a wall panel, probably of wattle and daub. The third phase was twice as big, with ten buildings spread across the ridge (see p.56). For these buildings, the wall supports, two rows of vertical planks with clear evidence of stake holes between them, were in foundation trenches (see plan below). The wattle work of the wall plates would have been formed round the upright stakes. The corners had additional timbers and the wall plate, where it met the roof, was supported by sloping timbers which allowed the archaeologists to estimate the height of the walls.

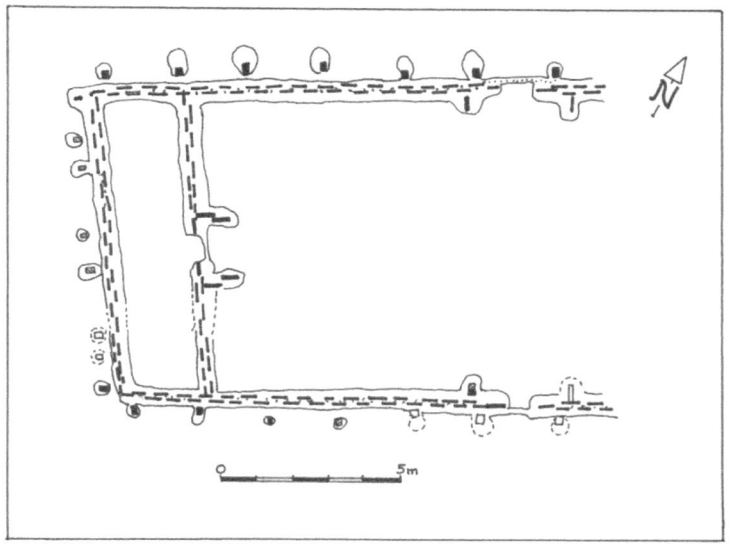

Plan of the structural evidence for building C12, Cowdery's Down, south west half (redrawn by A. Turton from Millett & James, 1983)

The whole structural evidence illustrates carpentry of the highest skill and a very liberal use of timber. There were partitions in some of the halls giving separate spaces, but the implication is that mostly they were communally occupied and of high status. There was very little evidence for farming or for any other use, very few items like pottery or animal bones were found. The site was remarkably clean! This fact, and the extravagance of the buildings, reinforces the interpretation of the settlement as being a noble, even possibly a royal site.

The size and complexity of building C12 in particular, which at over 22 metres long and almost 9 metres wide, would have been visible from some distance on the crest of the hill (now a green space behind Lambs Row) has led to comparisons with Yeavering, a known royal site in what was then the kingdom of Northumbria. This was the period when petty kings and warlords ruled over the territory they could control, often moving from site to site, much as medieval royalty did. It made sense to move to the stores of perishable supplies and consume them there rather than transport them to a central place, and it gave them the opportunity to conduct local business such as legal affairs. All the accoutrements of status – weapons, hearth furniture, textiles, tableware, all kinds of wooden items – would have travelled with them.

Saxon pottery is not as well-fired as Roman pottery and does not survive well; the fragments which were found were of simple kitchen ware. Nevertheless, Cowdery's Down was certainly the most impressive settlement in the village up to Saxon times so far discovered.

An artist's reconstruction of the last phase of the Cowdery's Down settlement based on the ground plan (Mike Codd, courtesy of Hampshire Cultural Trust)

Old Basing, of course, is one of the place names which are reckoned to denote early Saxon settlement. The followers of Basa settled here and it is possible that the name could have applied to Cowdery's Down which flourished between AD 600 and AD 800. However, there is some evidence of activity on the other side of the valley where the present village developed. A stray find of a Saxon cloak clip was found in Park Lane, and more convincingly, Saxon pottery at Basing House. During the excavations of the later earthworks on the site, such as the entrance to the Norman ringwork, there was a quantity of residual Saxon pottery (with the Iron Age and Roman material), (Allen & Anderson, 1999). This prominent position would have been a good choice for these later settlers. Also in the area close to the church, one or two burials have been radiocarbon dated to the 7th century (King & Cole, 2016), so they would have known the site at Cowdery's Down. At least two individuals, one a female, another a young adult, were found in graves in footings during the building of the Infant School. A much corroded iron implement was also recovered which looks convincingly like a scramasax, the usual form of Saxon knife (King & Cole, ibid.).

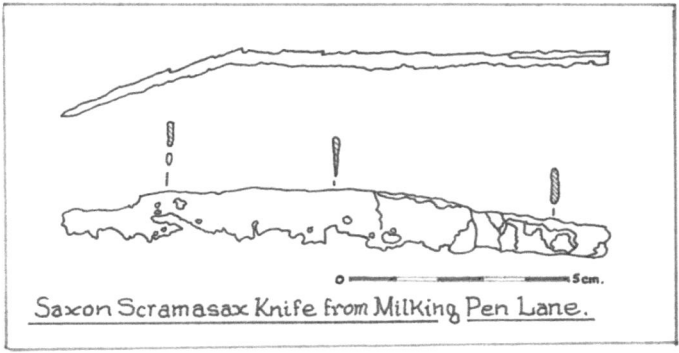

*Saxon scramasax knife from Milkingpen Lane
(redrawn by A. Turton from King & Cole, 2016)*

Just beyond the churchyard, the remains of two adult males were found, again during building work. It is tempting to think that there was a cemetery here, close to the predecessor of the present church. There is sufficient evidence to propose that there was a settlement where the village now stands. The houses may have been like those excavated at Chalton, and reconstructed at Butser Ancient Farm (see p.58).

Two experimental reconstructions at Butser Ancient Farm of a Saxon house (photo by P. Potter, courtesy of Butser Ancient Farm)

It is also possible that Oliver's Battery, which has not been excavated and is a protected site, and which is interpreted as an early motte and bailey castle built by the Normans, may have had an earlier phase during the Saxon period, as it is in a good position to defend the river crossing close to the Roman road. It could well have replaced Cowdery's Down as the stronghold of the local leader. It might explain why we had a 'battle in Basing'. The village name enters the historical record for certain in AD 871 in the Anglo Saxon Chronicle when this battle is recorded between the Danes and the Saxons. There is also later documentary evidence that Old Basing was royal property, but maybe it was already so which would have drawn the invaders to attack (Hinton, 1986). The site of the 'Battle of Basing' is not known, but is traditionally said to have taken place south of the A30 near Dickens Lane. It is just as possible they were fighting for local control around Oliver's Battery, where there might have been supplies worth fighting for. It was a victory for the Danes. However, the Saxons were led by King Aethelred and his younger brother Alfred. When the king died soon after, Alfred took the throne and successfully defended the kingdom over the following decades by a combination of military strength, ingenuity and diplomacy. He is the only English king to be called 'Great'.

With the establishment of Old Basing in its current location, it seems appropriate to close this account of the early story of the village. As recent work has shown, there will be many more discoveries and more information to add as more evidence is uncovered. The story continues!

Sources and further reading

General / various periods

The County Sites and Monuments record, now known as the Historic Environment Record (HER), gives the location and a summary of all the archaeological sites in the county and can be interrogated by grid reference. It is available online at https://maps.hants.gov.uk/historicenvironment/

The Portable Antiquities Scheme (PAS) is a record of chance finds of small items, often by metal detectorists, which have greatly enhanced the distribution maps of finds. The exact locations are not always revealed, but there is a description and usually a date, accessible online at https://finds.org.uk/

In the following list, '*Proceedings of the Hampshire Field Club & Archaeological Society*' is abbreviated to '*Proc. HFC*'.

Allen, D and Anderson, S, 1999. *Basing House Hampshire Excavations 1978-1991*, Hampshire Field Club and Archaeological Society Monograph 10, Bristol

Grainger, G, 1983. The Human Bone, in Millet, M and James, S, Excavations at Cowdery's Down, Basingstoke, Hampshire, 1978-81, *Archaeological Journal*, Vol 140, 151-279

Hey, G and Hind, J, 2014. *Solent-Thames Research Framework for the Historic Environment*, Oxford: Oxford Archaeology, Oxford Wessex Monograph, Vol 6

King, J and Cole, G, 2016. Radiocarbon Dating of Human Remains from Seven Sites in North Hampshire, *Proc. HFC*, Vol 71, 76-88

Millett, M and James, S, 1983. Excavations at Cowdery's Down, Basingstoke, Hampshire, 1978-81, *Archaeological Journal*, Vol 140, 151-279

Millett, M and Schadla-Hall, T, 1991. Rescue excavations on a Bronze Age and Romano-British site at Daneshill, Basingstoke 1980-81, *Proc. HFC,* Vol 47, 83-105

Pringle, G, 2020. Settlement and social and economic patterns at Old Basing, Hampshire: the results of a community archaeology project, *Proc. HFC*, Vol 75, 273-322

Stokes, E, 2008. *The Making of Basingstoke*, (eds. Applin, R & B), Basingstoke Archaeological & Historical Society

Wright, J, Powell, A B and Barclay, A, 2009. *Excavation of Prehistoric and Romano-British Sites at Marnel Park and Merton Rise (Popley) Basingstoke, 2004-8*, Salisbury: Wessex Archaeology Limited

Prehistoric

Allen, M J, Morris, M and Clark, R H, 1995. Food for the Living: a Reassessment of a Bronze Age Barrow at Buckskin, Basingstoke, Hampshire, *Proceedings of the Prehistoric Society*, Vol 61, 157-189

Annable, F K and Simpson, D D A, 1964. *Guide Catalogue of the Neolithic and Bronze Age Collections in Devizes Museum*, Wiltshire Archaeological & Natural History Society, Devizes

Ellaway, J R and Willis, G W, 1920. Field Notes - Basingstoke District, *Papers & Proceedings of the Hampshire Field Club*, Vol 9, 284-7

Ellaway, J R and Willis, G W, 1934. Field Notes - Basingstoke District, *Papers & Proceedings of the Hampshire Field Club*, Vol 12, 309-10

Oram, R, 2006. A Middle Bronze Age Burnt Mound at Greywell Road, Hatch, Basingstoke, *Proc. HFC*, Vol 61, 1-15

Peryer, M, 2016. The Investigation of a Burnt Mound at Greywell Moors, *Hampshire Field Club & Archaeological Society Newsletter*, No 65, 17-8

Roe, D A, 1968. *A gazetteer of British Lower & Middle Palaeolithic sites*, CBA Research Report No 8

Stevens, J, 1889. Early British Cemetery at Dummer, Hants (Paper read to British Archaeological Association on Nov. 21 1888), *British Archaeological Association*, Vol XLV, 112-22

Iron Age into Roman

Allen, M and Boothroyd, J, 2020. A Late Iron Age/Early Roman enclosed settlement at Basing View, Basingstoke, *Proc. HFC*, Vol 75, 191-219

Applebaum, S, 1953. The Distribution of the Romano-British Population in the Basingstoke Area, *Papers and Proc. HFC*, Vol 18, 119-138

Bristow, J and Harrap, P, 2024. Archaeology Section Conference, 18 November 2023 'What we've done and what we've found', *Hampshire Field Club & Archaeological Society Newsletter*, No 81, 2-5

Combley, R C, Notman, J W and Pike, H H M, 1966. Further Excavations at Basing House, 1964-66, *Proc. HFC*, Vol 23, Part 3, 96-109

Fulford, M, 2021. *Silchester Revealed: The Iron Age and Roman Town of Calleva*, Windgather Press

Lalor, B A, 2015. The Iron Age and Romano-British Enclosures at Lamb's Field, Worting: Excavations by the Basingstoke Archaeological and Historical Society, 1992-2008, *Proc. HFC*, Vol 70, 41-62

Lyne, M and Jefferies, R, 1979. *The Alice Holt/Farnham Roman Pottery Industry*, London: Council for British Archaeology, CBA Research Report 30

Millett, M and Russell, D, 1984. An Iron Age and Romano-British Site at Viables Farm, Basingstoke, *Proc. HFC*, Vol 40, 49-60

Oliver, M, Anderson, F W, Bird, J, Mays, S A and Murphy, P, 1992. Excavation of an Iron Age and Romano-British Settlement Site at Oakridge, Basingstoke, Hampshire 1965-1966, *Proc. HFC*, Vol 48, 55-94

Oliver, M and Applin, B, 1978. Excavation of an Iron Age and Romano-British Settlement at Ructstalls Hill, Basingstoke, Hampshire, *Proc. HFC*, Vol 35, 41-92

Pringle, V, 2014. Continuity and Change: a study of Late Bronze Age and Iron Age settlement patterns at the head of the Loddon valley, North Hampshire, unpublished thesis, University of Winchester

Sanigar, J and Andrews, P, 2020, 'Late Iron Age-Romano British settlement at Razor's Farm, Chineham, Basingstoke', *Proc. HFC*, Vol 75, 220-54

Smith, K, 1977. The excavation of Winklebury Camp, Basingstoke, Hampshire, *Proceedings of the Prehistoric Society*, Vol 43, 31-129

Saxon

Alcock, N W and Walsh, D, 1993, Architecture at Cowdery's Down: A Reconsideration, *Archaeological Journal* 150, 403-9

Hinton, D A, 1986. The place of Basing in mid-Saxon history, *Proc. HFC*, Vol 42 162-4

Mary Oliver is the author of:

Church Cottage Basingstoke (2008)

Excavation of an Iron Age and Romano-British settlement site at Oakridge, Basingstoke, Hampshire, 1965-1966
(Proceedings of the Hampshire Field Club Archaeological Society, 1992, Vol 48)
(co-authors F.W. Anderson, J. Bird, S.A. Mays, P. Murphy)

Excavation of an Iron Age and Romano-British Settlement at Ructstalls Hill, Basingstoke, Hampshire
(Proceedings of the Hampshire Field Club Archaeological Society, 1978 Vol 35)
(co-author B. Applin)